A REQUIEM FOR LOVE

A REQUIEM FOR LOVE

CALVIN MILLER

AUTHOR OF *THE SINGER* TRILOGY

WORD PUBLISHING
Dallas · London · Sydney · Singapore

A REQUIEM FOR LOVE

Library of Congress Cataloging-in-Publication Data

Miller, Calvin.
    A requiem for love / Calvin Miller.
        p.   cm.
    ISBN 0-8499-0687-3
    I. Title.
PS3563.I376R47   1989
811'.54—dc19   89-30734
                                            CIP

Printed in the United States of America
9801239 AGF 987654321

Other books in the
"Symphony" Trilogy will be:
A Symphony in Sand
An Overture of Light

A
REQUIEM
FOR LOVE

No serpent ever crawled so low
He did not dream of thrones and
    crowns.

I

He came like loving wind
And left the sand astir behind Him.
The desert burned in early sun
As He approached the towering gates,
Knowing they would open at His word.

He knew His hissing foe would be there,
Brilliant gold and scarlet evil,
Yellow-eyed with old, diminished hope.
The serpent spoke, rising from his coiled form,
Straining for a glimpse inside the gates.
He longed to know what wonders
His almighty enemy was fashioning
Beyond the boundaries of evil.
He saw . . . and yet saw nothing.
One hurried blur of shimmering greens
That mocked the starving sands
The serpent called his kingdom.

"Welcome to your Garden, Eminence,"
The rising reptile hissed.
Earthmaker turned,
"Slithe, once-loved, once crowned
Can this be you,
Self-damned, condemned to sand?"

Slithe laughed.
"Lock me from the green; it is only for a while.
Full well you know, I *will* be in."

"Once the entire universe was yours.
You chose these desert chains."

"I chose a throne and got the chains,"
The serpent spewed his bitter grudge.

The Father-Spirit turned toward the gates
As they swung slowly open.
His old accuser blinked into the distant splendor.
"Will You succeed this time
In fashioning a lover
Who will remain a lover?
Or, is Your new creation
Destined to betray You?
Why are You forever
Planting hope in high-walled gardens?"

The Father-Spirit looked away.
"Terra holds this Sanctuary as a dream
Where love abused by treachery
May mold a masterpiece of hope.
Today I crown all I have ever made
And honor Terra's clay by stamping it *Imago Mei*,
A man, a prince—Regis, friend of spirit.
He shall wear the crown of love you cast aside.
But you shall never see his coronation,
For only perfect love shall pass these gates."

"Has this new creature, gift of choice?
Can this Regis, Prince of Terra,
Bid me enter, or is he just a puppet
Stringed hand and foot to Your almighty fingers?
Does he dance to Your enslaving orders,
Obeying You, daring nothing on his own?
Obey . . . Now there's a word for you. . .
Obey . . . A scab on freedom . . . A collar and
   a chain,
An insult to all dignity. Will you tell him
As you call him into life,
'Obey Me, Regis, and I'll love you
But if you're naughty, out you go!'
Has he will, I ask You?"

The Father-Spirit smiled.
The huge gates swung fully open now, exposing
      Sanctuary.
"Behold, low Serpent-King, what you can never
      have . . .
I'm going in now. This day is triumph
For the Masterpiece is done!
And I will soon en-spirit him with being.
Man shall be born and stand a king today!"

"He shall be Regis, lover of his Maker.
Man made to cherish truth, and bless the morning
      sun—
Valor with a dream, bold to excise evil—
Chaste love and high compassion,
Heaping dignity on all he touches!
Man shall devote himself to beauty and to art.
Knowledge will be treasure unto him
Giving birth to science.
And with science he shall widen all this shining
      place
Till My garden claims your barren realm."

Made miserable by all he'd lost,
The serpent spat out venom.
"Your dream is proof of error!"
"Almighty in naïveté is what You are.
Go ahead . . . .
Close these gates that shut out nothing!
If Regis has the slightest will,
I'll smash his chain and set him free.
And Your weak and foolish Prince
Will give his crown, at last, to me!
Will You never learn, Earthmaker?
There are no walled retreats—
No soul that does not yearn
To know the sweet forbidden.
The freedom that You always give

Becomes at last the very weapon
That we level at Your heart."

Slithe slithered close to the grand gates.
With the desert at his back, he sang
A haunting chant of despair.

"He is born today . . . man who comes to nothing!
His bloody soul will murder peace
And he shall mine the earth for swords and spears
Till Earthmaker's noble dreams lie still
In rotting battlefields.
Man, the grisly joke Earthmaker plays upon Himself.
Man, the vicious image of his Maker,
Blinding birds to make them sing,
Chaining kindred men to make them slaves,
Gouging Terra's fields with avarice,
Burying himself in bulging-eyed excesses.

Great Earthmaker, must I tell You what You know?
Man will not follow truth nor worship art,
He will follow what his greed shall nominate,
Leave his children begging life from wolves.
Crown his appetites till gluttony is queen
And lust is king, ruling
His degenerate kingdom from a soiled bed.
Today, when You en-spirit him with life
And make him free to choose,
You dare not tell him that
There is a Serpent in the desert.
For if man knows that I exist,
His appetite to have all that is forbidden
Will splinter these tall gates, crying out to evil,
'Come in, O come . . . I've learned too narrowly!'
I've only then to sleep, and when I wake
Your eagle will leave sky to be a snake."

The gates clanged shut.

Life found itself alive
And somehow knew its opposite was
    death.
We are ever being born, or dying,
And the thrill of choosing is
    ours.
Only once, must we be born without
    our own consent.
Only once, must we die without our
    own permission.

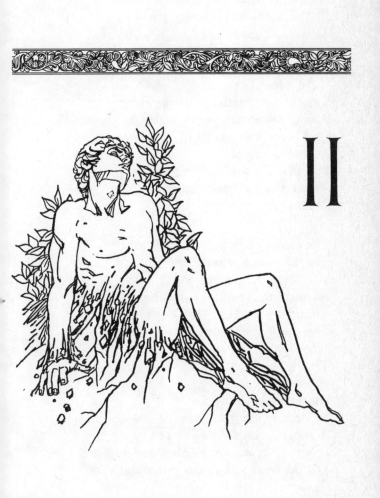

II

Inside the high, closed gates
The Father-Spirit walked,
Silent in the leafy temples
Of man's birthing altar.
Earthmaker made His way
To a sylvan grotto
Where His sleeping sculpture waited.
Spirit stared at flesh, exulting!
"Live, Man!
Receive the breath to call me 'Father'!
And the sweetness of the name shall honor Me.
And I shall call you 'Son'—
And the glory of that name shall honor you.
I breathe My spirit into you
As benediction over manhood.
Be sovereign over Sanctuary!"

The eyes grew bright with life,
The noble head raised regally.
The dry earth cracked and fell away,
As music broke—like lightning, and
Thunder pealed in Spirit-laughter.
The clay-made creature stood!
"Move and grow in understanding."
The Father-Spirit spoke.
"I give you Terra
Glistening in sunlight.
Stones and earth and mist,
A pool that calls your face a twin.
Feather, fur, and fang—claw, and fingernail.
Sky, distance, leaf, blade, green, and blue."

The new prince studied his new world,
And staring at all that was made,
He saw the great unseeable.
His emotions reached,

Growing, swelling as he realized
He was in love not with what was merely made,
But with the lavish Maker of so rich a world.
"Spirit, intangible! I am wrapped in new passion
Lost in first-being.
Here upon this planet I have found myself alive,
And best of all the friend of Earthmaker.
Father-Spirit, I am made today nobility, high-born,
Crowned rich with Grace!
I LOVE YOU!"

"Father, Maker of myself,
I join these gentle zephyrs
That stir the ferns to praise!
I bless the creature eyes that peer
Through forest walls.
Listen now, glad heart,
To swirling wingbeats.
See the silver fire that leaps from fin
To mirrored lake
And sleeps in shimmering promises.

The naked Prince laid down in the grass
Soaking life from Terra's ochre soil.
"Son!" Earthmaker breathed the gallant word,
Soft and often as the breeze that
Whispered oaks alive.
"Gift unto Myself—
The Prince of presence—
Lest I should ever be alone.
Now, Regis, image of My Being,
You are the Child
To brighten My lonely house
And the glad resolution to My years inside Myself."

The new man listened, overcome by Presence.
To be given all the world at once,
Stopped his tongue

And left his wit too dead for words.
Overwhelmed, he broke the awesome quiet.
"Father, I receive Your gift of being, but
You have made me *too* rich
To name my wealth
And yet too poor
To give You anything of meaning.
I love with only giftless love."

"Regis, there is no such thing as 'giftless' love.
The very words accuse each other.
My gift to you is love, but
Worship is your gift to Me.
And Oh, most glorious it is!
Worship always calls Me 'Father' and
Makes us both rich with a common joy.
Worship Me, for only this great gift
Can set you free from the killing love of self,
And prick your fear with valiant courage
To fly in hope through moments of despair.
Worship will remind you
That no man knows completeness in himself.
Worship will teach you to speak your name,
When you've forgotten who you are.
Worship is duty and privilege,
Debt and grand inheritance at once.
Worship, therefore, at those midnights
When the stars hide.
Worship in the storms till love
Makes thunder whimper and grow quiet
And listen to your whispered hymns.
Worship and be free."
A sparrow darted in between them
Its brown-gold flash of feathers
Stopped in the Father-Spirit's hand.

"Here," said Earthmaker, "is your sister.
Life not so high as yours—

Nor yet aware of its own separate self,
But sacred!"

Regis took the bird.
And held it in his hand,
Stroked it and released it.
It flew away.

"Tell me all of life and love,"
The Earth-born Regent pled.

"In time . . . In time.
For now, let life and love be one.
As I have ever been . . ."

"But I have not . . ."

"Deny not, Regis, how long you've lived.
In the misty, deep and unmarked
Crevasses of time, you have always lived
In the very vastness of My heart
As the waiting portrait of My eternal being."

The Spirit and His shining creature,
Encircled hearts and drew themselves to
        union . . .
Being in embrace . . . Creature and Creator
So in love that the sky and breeze declared it!
"Father, is love forever?"

"It may be, son . . . It may be!
Only worship Me, and you shall see
That love will name itself infinity!"

To be touched tells man that he is
    loved.
To touch tells man that he is lover.
Touching is therefore, being
Tango ergo sum!
I touch; therefore, I am!

III

The Father-Spirit was not there
When the crimson morning came
And His absence filled
His waking son with restless emptiness.
For one bright day and spangled night,
His lover did not come.
Regis' heart was set in quest.
By day and night he looked
But neither sun nor moon would speak
Nor disclose the hiding place of God.
"Father!" he called and reached
Up to the thin blue of pale day.
There was no answer.
The sky did not brighten,
The breeze whispered nothing!
"Father, Father . . . . " he called once more.
The quiet grew with greater absence.
"Your world is here, but where are You?
Speak . . . O speak . . . for if You are not here,
Mere created beauty is throatless and purpose deaf.
Where are You, Father?
I have searched the emptiness
And cried out to the mocking stars,
'Where is Love, if He is not?'"

An immediate longing that he could not stem
Washed over him and left him feeling more alone.
His solitary oneness was rebuked by nature's
        "two-ness."
Two doves, white as first light, fluttered past him.
Two deer drank from a nearby pool.
The stag and doe were different
And yet they walked together
In complementing oneness—
So with the cock and hen,
The bruin and his mate.

"All life in Sanctuary comes in twos but mine.
I alone walk in solitude."
Regis' oneness stained his joy with doubt.

In the passing of the days,
Regis often woke entangled in the issue
Of his oneness.
He felt empty—separated
Somehow from all that lived—
Needing something so elusive
It would not define itself!

Yet, if no mate, he had a Father.
Suddenly he felt ashamed because he felt alone
And then he felt alone because he felt ashamed.
Each time he put it from his mind, to think of it
      no more,
The stag and doe would pass again,
And their "two-ness" woke his yearning solitude.

Once wading in a mirrored pool
He suddenly stood still.
Staring down at his reflection.
He cried out to his inner soul,
"If I step from this pool
I'll be alone again."
When Regis knelt to bring his image near
Just the moving of his body
Wrinkled water and cut his face
Into a hurried set of silver ribbons.
He left the pool at last,
Certain that the water's mimicry
Only scoffed at his need.

"O Father-Spirit, come,"
He begged, "Come, Come . . .
I am lonely . . . it is not good.
For loneliness grieves, in starving solitude,

Desperate for stars to talk.
Loneliness is wandering in want,
Making richness poor,
And rendering earth's music tuneless.
Loneliness leaves dancing bound in melancholy."
His words died in empty wind.
An eagle, in the cold sky, screamed!
And Regis stared into the deep abyss
Of despairing oneness,
And for the first time formed
The dark words, "Who am I?"

Hearing the ache in Regis' soul,
The Father-Spirit came at last.

"Consort to Myself,
Reflection of My glory
Are we not two?"

"Not two, but one. I am alone.
Where were You, Father?
I needed You . . ." Regis wept.

"Here! Wherever your eye fell, I was!"

"I couldn't see You . . . You didn't speak!"

"I am here, always . . . In looking for Me, you but
        looked through me.
I spoke a thousand times . . . Did you not hear
        the eagle scream?
The rumbling of the waterfalls?
The songs of nightingales
And clarions of wild rams?"

"How can I know You when You hide,
For even if You speak and hang transparent in the air
Spirit cannot reach with fingers

Firm enough to touch.
Nothing in my world embraces me with nearness.
In my aloneness I find the forest far too wide—
The world too open."

A finch darted to a small nest
And with her feathered mate
Snuggled into tightness.
"See how all the creatures, each one touch
And draw themselves to glorious
Togetherness . . . and life . . . "

"No, Regis,
See the glory that we are!
These creatures are but gentle celebrants of power.
Their tiny glory applauds My creativity
And yet they cannot frame
The smaller meaning that is theirs.
You alone are King of all that I have made,
And Kings wear being as the heavy crown of
        self-awareness.
To be troubled over who you are
Is glory more unspeakable
Than these small creatures can conceive.
It is not their hearts
Only their wingbeats that praise,
'Earthmaker is!'"

"Why then," Regis began,
"Do I yearn to see the open world
Close tighter all around me?"

"Come, Son, despair no more!"
His gentle Father led him
To a grotto altar, edged by thick, concealing ferns.
There, in terra cotta
Lay a silent form begging life.
"Here is she who shall

Complete your need."
Regis bowed his head.
Her beauty reached inward and stirred
A kind of reverence he had never felt before.
She seemed alive, asleep,
About to rise.
He studied the softness in her face,
Her eyes were closed, and yet he sensed
That they were windows waiting to be opened
        unto life.
His eyes fell on her waiting hands
Promising touch.
Suddenly he loved! The emotion flew at him!
He felt it from the inside moving outward,
Rising with power and soul need.
"Father," he breathed,
And his breath was nearly prayer.
"This is my need, beckoning me to nearer
        worship—
At last, a love that touches flesh with flesh!
Let her lie no longer
Begging breath and pulse!"
He paused reflectively, then asked,
"Why only now have You shown this perfect answer
To my emptiness?"

"I gave you yearning oneness
To define your need.
In your hungering to be touched
You found out who you were."

Regis reached out to the clay-dead form.
"Oh, bid her live for me
As lionness to lion,
As stag to doe,
As sire to dame,
As intimacy and all of hope."

"I will . . . but Son . . . first gaze in wonder,
And study all she is—
Dim time beyond the light of vision
Will teach all later ages her full worth!
She is woman, *Gloriana*
In excellence created.
See the face of love!

"Behold her!
Woman, being from man's side.
Liberated from harsh manliness,
Given wisdom unto motherhood,
Tenderness, for her calling as a wife . . .
Music for the lullabies that shall teach her little
      ones to sleep with courage . . .
Strength for lonely widowhood, if life should
      brutalize.
Her power will be in seeing all your fast moving
      eyes shall miss.
She will feel the pain you hurry past.
She will move in gentle inwardness, that sees
      so often
Past your logic-driven days.
Call her 'Woman'!
Give her honor!
Lift her up,
And she will grow secure,
And protected by your affirmation,
She will school you in self worth!"

"Behold and reach!
Touch the sunlight on her hair,
For hair is woman's glory,
Born to you as gold.
These eyes shall look on you with glad esteem,
Bidding love be born.

"Come touch these fragile arms and hands,
Made strong as service,
For she, like you, is made to serve.
These breasts are for the nourishing of life.
Here future sons of yours shall feed.
Here is her body, fertile with possibility.
Rich with power to create life—
Here we three shall one day meet
And the issue from her being shall be glorious.
'Nation' is a word that time will understand
But you and she shall one day make this planet laugh
With continents of children, needing love and
    celebrating joy.
Thus, worshiping Myself, Terra shall know
    purpose."

"Oh, let her live! Give sinew to this clay."
"In time . . . In time . . . ," His Father
    soft-replied,
"My Spirit shall indwell your sleeping bride."

Eden was the birthing room
Of all of modern knowledge.
There darksome sociology was born.
How shall we define
This old, unsettled science?
As homeless Homo Sapiens
Picking apples in the dark
So the orchard owner cannot see.

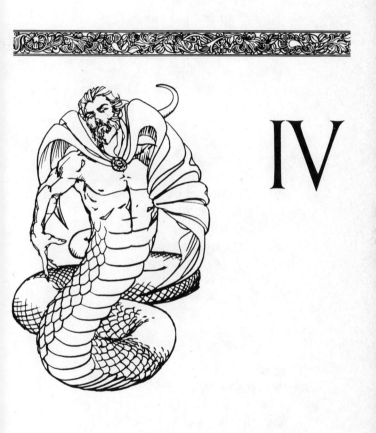

IV

Once again the World Hater
Met Earthmaker near
The gates of Sanctuary.
As before, Earthmaker swirled in spiraled wind
That skittered air and twisted sand toward heaven.
"Today I give them the glorious gift
Of love's full ecstasy," He said.

Through the foaming dust
The serpent glided toward the whirlwind.
"You know where the gift
Of human loving
Will one day take the race.
Dare You trust them with a gift
So easily misgiven, so often uncontrolled?
Such love will only seem their friend.
In truth, it shall rise as pale lust
Bloodless in neural fire
Which shall order them to fury
Till they lie, spent in shallow oneness,
Powerless in the spell of appetites
That fettered them to passion.
Poor creatures . . . children of a devious Father
Who gives them scorpions as gifts!

"A Father whose loving children
Need to touch, but cannot do it
Without summoning destruction—
Think You, that they will worship You,
When their eyes are eager with desire?"

The snake glided to a stone
Already warmed by sunlight.
And the Father-Spirit watched,
As the Serpent changed himself
Into a man.

"See, even I am man enough
To summon fire
And call Prince Regis' bride
To lie with me and widen knowledge.
You know the end of Eros!
Keep human rapture to yourself
Or, at least, don't call it gift!
Give them rather hemlock
And let them die believing that
Human ecstasy is nobler than it is."

"My gifts are ever right," Earthmaker thundered.
"And what I give to both My children
Shall nourish them with close dependence.
This gift is fire, to forge
Their closeness when the night is cold.
Intimacy is its name
And righteousness, its bond.
They will lift it as the treasure
Of their union—
Divinely given flame,
To warm not burn
Nor ever rage in selfishness.
They shall receive this gift in gratitude,
And worship Me for giving it."

"Worship in the midst of lust—Hah!
They shall abuse, not use, this gift.
Their need for You will be swallowed whole
In eager, vulgar hunger."
The Father-Spirit left the desert,
And the shrieking Slithe,
For He would no longer listen to
His blasphemy of human loving.

So stepping into Sanctuary,
The Father whispered wisdom on the breeze.
"My children, Regis and Regina,

Regents of primeval Terra,
I bring you both a gift
That shall endow you with
Strong dreams of love's posterity.
You shall live on through this gift
Eternal in your children,
Eternal in My love!
But . . . beware,
Teach this gift discipline,
Let it never ever feed capriciously
Eating what it will and when.
You must not ever take the gift beyond your union,
Or offer it, uncherished, to any cheaper use.
If it wanders curiously afield,
Remind it of its Giver,
And bid it mind its pure intent.
Two are the keepers of this gift.
For three, it holds obscenity and death.
Be born in splendor and esteem the night,
Your loving shall be king, not appetite."

It is the eye that bids the fingers reach.
It is the touching finger that
Calls its parent-hand to grasp and
    hold.
But, grasping kills all
That the eye at first desired.
So touch is strong narcotic,
Begging lovers to an addiction.

V

Wind twisted into clay,
And the clay received it
As the breath of its Creator.
"Live!" howled the laughing
Gales of life.

The Queen, effused by Spirit,
Rose and gazed, as color
Baptized her sight in splendor.
"Daughter . . . " said the Father,
"Set your feet upon the Earth,
And make it tremble
With the imperial authority
Of first existence.
You are born today,
And bring a double crown to both of us.
Your crown is human being.
My crown is instant Fatherhood.
Live and bless us both."

He thrilled to watch her first steps.
She waved her hands low, sideward,
As though the gentle fanning of the air
Would balance her tremulous uprightness.
Timidly, the woman-child walked,
The loving wind held Spirit-hands
To keep her from falling as she
Straightened then and moved
From fear to purpose,
As learning child to strident Empress
In but a score of steps.

"I love you, Daughter . . .
But linger not so near your birthing altar.
My lonely Son is waiting,
Dreaming of your coming.

Go and offer him
The gift of human loving,
And you shall teach
This living planet Grace!"

She walked as dignity to coronation
While, unknowing, the Prince of Terra waited.

The trees rose stiff and tall, erect, remote.
Regis stood and looked away,
Again alone . . . alone . . . alone.
Till suddenly, beauty seared his vision.
He was like a child who, staring at the sun,
Is blinded by the brilliance.

Across the meadow where the
World fell into tangled green—
He saw her once again,
Only now—she lived—
Earth-molded woman—
Glorious in sunlight!
Making Sanctuary rich!

The woman's shadow fell ahead of her
And drew her forward toward the man.
She must know him and be with him
And yet she walked in measured steps,
For she had only come to be
And while asking who she was
She now must ask who he was, too.
Drawn by her face, he, also,
Walked slow with wider stride,
Afraid a hurried pace would wipe away
The lovely apparition and leave him lonely
        once again.
"Be born at last my vision!
Did ever eye know light till now?"
Breathed Regis and then in wild elation,

He shouted to his living, standing queen,
"Reign with me over earth,
And for your missing throngs of subjects
Take myself—I genuflect before
The royal promise of my Father
Who fills, at last, my need
With such completeness,
I am near to song."

Despairing with a madness given to mirage, they met
At last, like hesitant gazelles in fertile meadows.
They reached with stretching fingertips
Until their threadlike souls were fused
And their joy fell in utter weakness.
Hand gathered fingers into hand.
Eye locked into eye.
They stood while joy rose upward
Through the ground, effusing them with such
        exuberance
Their hypnotic drunkenness must burst
At once in ecstasy!
He turned and so did she.
They ran in glorious two!
Like harts or wildebeests
They fell in laughter in new meadows
And rolled like newborn colts.

"Regis, I am born today along
With love," Regina cried.
"Oh, hold me now as mooring for my spirit
Lest I should rise in rapture
Never more to touch the earth."

Lip brushed eager lip—
Their bodies trembling
In the breeze-kissed forest, touched.
Terra blessed the warmth of

First love.
Closeness folded over in glorious assurance.
And then for reasons which knew no reason—
They broke in gales of running laughter
That joined the frothing melodies of nearby brooks.
The hush of first life gave way
To gentle conversation.
"Are we alone—the two of us?"
Her question answered by the asking,
Slid soundless into waxy leaves,
Dissolved in green, and flew at rising mist.

She pried at his reluctance to break the reverie,
"What did you do before I came?"

"I waited . . . but impatiently," he answered.

"For me?"

"For . . . two . . . for love!"

"And did your Father Spirit not love you?"

"He did and does . . .
You're here because He loves!
I waited and lamented that His
Love was incomplete somehow.
Our Father is all-wise.
He knew exactly what I needed
Before I knew enough to ask."

"Then why did He withhold me
And leave you so alone?"

"Because loneliness is the brooding parent
Of becoming—thought and busy being
Seldom come together.

Regina, He is a gentle lover
Whose glorious love is a gentle teacher.

"And can I meet this Father-Lover?"

"You cannot escape *that* joy!
In every sunrise you will meet Him.
Put any blossom to your ear
And it will whisper love's full name.
You will meet our Father
A thousand times each day you live.
He thrusts Himself as oak to sky.
Hangs out the lights of night
That twinkle to assure us
He is here—As life is here."

"I see Him even now
Within your eyes—
His glory lights your hair.
His warmth is in your touch.
His trust walks in your footprints.
His power calls me to give my body
To your keeping
As He gave you to me.
Ask not if you shall meet Him.
He swims the air we breathe—
Inhabits light.
Unless your eyes should fail
And all your senses die,
You must meet *Him*, who can on any day,
Fashion love from ordinary clay."

A godless pilgrim wandered, searching.
Young, he first sought God among the
    roses;
Old and dim of eye, he looked among
    the stars
And cried with withered, empty hands
That never had held truth,
"Where can I find God?"
The crying wind replied,
"Only at the seam of mud and mystery
Where spirit marries flesh."

VI

Sit here," said the Man.
"Lean back against my chest."
He felt her hair like flaxen
Filaments of glory
Fashioned into richness
By the blazing, fading sun.
"By all He is, I love you.
Come Father-Spirit,
Bless our joyous oneness with Your presence."

The Father-Spirit came,
"Children, formed by My own spirit fingers,
I bless you."

"Father?" Regina softly asked.
"Who was Your maker?
What world was Sanctuary unto You?"

Earthmaker pointed outward into space,
As an upward draft of wind
That lifts a floating leaf to sky,
"I come from where
There is no coming—I walked
The pathless paths of unborn universe.
Before I taught the light its radiance.
I knew the night of nothingness
While still it hungered for the warmth of worlds.
Now, you, My children,
Crown My universe with meaning.
You yearn for truth
As cold yearns to be warm,
And dark lusts after light.
Oh, at last, my empty Terra
Knows her dwelling place!"

The three then walked
Until at last they stood between two trees.

Here the Father-Spirit, elusive as a breeze
Spoke into the stillness.
"Between these trees lies great responsibility.
Here you must remember who you are
And treasure our relationship.
Hold to all you honor.
The fruit of these two trees
Shall be your burden.
The fruit of one is morning,
Blessing you with rich unending day.
The fruit of the other is sunset,
Dark with the nectar of destruction.
Eat of morning and bless our love.
Eat of sunset, and you will soon love only
   things.
Then craving power, you will turn from service
And broken trust will devour our oneness.

"Despair not—but remember
All being knows a heaviness of burden.
I, too, must bear a burden.
I took it up when I created you
And made you free to choose.
My children, your Father, too, knows heaviness.
All being bears a weight
Proportioned to its size.
To stride these stars
With all that I must carry,
Would break the spine of spindling galaxies.

"I wanted you to be,
And yet I would not give you
Empty being . . . I made you free to choose,
Aware your choices might
Destroy all.

"To make lovers, who might at any time,
Become the fanged monsters

That spring at love and sting it with a poisonous
     treason,
Is my God-sized burden.

"Implanting love and choice in you
Is that heaviness which I must carry,
Staggering underneath the weight
Of what I've given.
I know at last My children might greet Me
With faithless daggers,
Stabbing Fatherhood—
Not killing it but wounding all its dreams.

"Choose carefully therefore, for,
Between the morning and the sunset of your
     choosing
You may discover
The Hater of this world.
He smashes planets, ruins stars . . .
Gives birth to hell in Heaven's midst.
Eat only for your appetite,
And you shall unleash his destructive evil
In this fair place."

For the first time in her brief, new life,
Naïveté parted like forking water,
And Regina saw choice as utter terror.
When every day held choices to be made,
Every choice was threatening with consequence.
She must choose good so quickly
She'd have no time to choose good's opposite.

"Is the Hater of this world in sanctuary?"
Asked the woman.

"He will be or may be.
The same desire which
Summoned Me will summon him."

"Never shall we summon him,"
Regina was firm . . . "Never"
And yet a twinge of curiosity
Touched her deeply and she wondered if
What she did not know
Was somehow *worth* the knowing.
The sunset smothered her in cold fatigue
As her desires now fondled new intrigue.

Hate never tells the truth convincingly
And Caesar's cry,
Et tu, Bruté,
Is always love
Reaching out to try to understand
Why trust cannot be trusted . . .
Why all our lovers carry daggers,
And why Judas kisses freely only
In Gethsemanes of need.

VII

The Prince of Sanctuary woke each day,
As one whose dreams would not let go of him.
The fullness of his love
Reached out to touch his queen.
To but see her was to want to touch her,
And to touch her, begged him hold her.
Love was so abundant and at hand,
He felt a stinging brightness in his own eyes,
When he but looked at his beloved.

One night within the glade
Where they had drawn
The garlands of their bower
About themselves, Regina asked,
"Is the World-Hater enemy
To all our Father loves?"

The man nodded.
"He is someone in this starry universe
Whom we will never meet."

"Still I am intrigued by all
I do not know of power.
What is power? What is it like?"

"I cannot say
But it lies opposite of our Father's love.
As love is sun, so craving power is ice.
As love creates, power may destroy.
As love makes one . . . power sometimes
        amputates
And divorces lovers by its unholy greed."

"Still," Regina wondered,
"Power, like love, may be a kind of knowing.

Oh, that I knew all that may be known."
Each looked away,
As though her words desired too much.

They said little else as daylight faded
But Regina slept—In restlessness
Stirring in their bower,
Waking only once in darkness
And crying to the night,
"Can love be love
Until it knows its opposite?"
She fell again to troubled sleep.

Regis sensed her discontent
When first light woke them both.
He led her from the glade
Unto the altar where both of them were born.
"Let us, here, where we both woke to light,
Kneel and remember how Almighty-love once
      fashioned our completeness
From the hungers of my solitude."
He paused, then bowed his head
And worshiped with a single word, "Father."
Regina worshiped with a single word . . . "Love."
Their simple act of reverence
Gave way to singing.
"The Father gave the world to us
And woke us with the Light of Love!"

The man then left off his praise,
Too full to speak, made mute by
Double ardor . . .
When his joy-choked voice returned
He spoke to both his Maker and his Queen,
"Twice-loved am I, and made so wealthy,
That I dare not choose which worship I should
      treasure most.

Give counsel every breeze to name priority,
Is love all wealth, and hate all poverty?
My Father's love is sky untouchable.
My woman's fair embrace is earth beneath.
My universe, thus framed with love is light,
Whose radiance is rich, forbidding night!"

Love smiles.
Hate grins.

VIII

Regina left the grotto
Of their worship.
She walked alone
And wondered what it would be like
To actually see
Her Father's enemy.
Her curiosity grew
Until she spoke almost aloud,
"O that I might see him . . ."
Her words were barely out
When she looked and saw,
lying by the water's edge,
A handsome youth—
The only man she'd ever seen
Besides her Prince and Lover.
She blurted out with trembling,
"Are you our enemy?"
Feeling both fear and enticement
She drew instantly away
And yet with reaching curiosity.

He grinned,
Then beckoned with his finger,
"Come, Queen, and know another King.
The wise replace their fear
With broader trust,
And make friends of every terror
That they feel.
I am Slithe, no enemy, but friend.
I'm ready now to serve your curiosity
And answer all your wonder.
There is power, Regina, in the things
That I can teach you.
For evil can be fair as love."
Slithe paused and smiled, then spoke again.
"How well I do remember love,

Simple, plain, single-hearted.
Indeed love once was all I knew
Before I chose to choose.
Your Father-Spirit told me then
That if I widened life past
That thin stingy living
Which He calls obedience,
I would despise
The consequences of my liberty.
But I was forged in freedom's foundry,
And could not live beneath
The thumb of all His threats
And His smothering demands for adoration.
I reached for power!
He slapped my hands!
Still I rose up to grab His scepter,
Telling Him that His tyranny
Was not liberty!
'Rule those content to be the mindless
Serfs of Your enslaving prohibitions!'
I struck at Him with honesty."

Slithe stopped and laughed,
"And then this tyrant you call Father,
Pitched me into space,
Telling me I'd die of disobedience.
But as you clearly see, I didn't.
In fact, I learned a glorious truth that day.
There is a wondrous option to His loving
      narrowness.
For having chosen on my own, I'm free of Him,
With all my visions richer for the choosing.

"He wept, they say, the first day that I hated,
And so, you see, my choosing taught us both."

Regina reached out timidly for logic,
"He bid us trust *Him*, Slithe . . . warning us that

There are things better left unchosen."
"You're not naked," Regina interrupted herself,
"As Prince Regis and myself."
Surprised as much that he was dressed
As that he had ever come to Sanctuary.

Slithe sneered.
"Did your Father-Spirit warn you even against
        clothes?
Did He tell you clothes are only covered nakedness?
It's so like Him to fail to mention
That clothes designate all classes,
Otherwise we gods would look like mortals
And souls of honor and dishonor would look alike.
Clothes hide every blemish on the soul
And mask the body in whatever pretense we desire.
Clothes give life wonder
Then give us to the world
As we would like the world to have us.
Tell me *your* nakedness is innocence.
Tell me you have not in heart already undressed
        myself,
Wondering, if gods and mortals look alike.
Your husband's eye need never wonder,
Nor spend a moment of intrigue on you.
Shamelessly you give the sun itself full cognizance."

His words made her feel ugly,
Created as a barren thing of shame.
Then suddenly she straightened!
Shouting at the leering god,
"Both I and love came full at once,
My Father made my world and me,
As both of us should be.
Stag and doe dress not,
Their innocence clothes them with that same
        dignity
That Regis and myself do wear.

"Be gone,
What need have I of clothes?
You were wrong to come . . . !"

"Wrong to come?" The World-Hater sneered.
"I'm here at your request.
Last night as you fell asleep
You longed for evil,
Even after you had worshiped.
How like humanity to worship truth
And cherish evil in the same moment.
Let's get things straight, I do not barge
Into any soul unwelcomed by the heart.
You voiced aloud your need to see me.
I granted you your desire, that's all.
You will surely long again
And I will come again,
For evil is seasonal within the human breast."

"If I can wish you here,
Then I can wish you elsewhere.
Begone!" She shouted once again, "Now!"

And Slithe was gone.

But where he stood,
She found the ground chilled—
The grass, crystalline with frost.
"The white is beautiful,"
She mused, intrigued. "It's strange,
Where hate *and* knowledge bend to touch the earth,
The heart may long for truth, but doubt its worth."

The greatest sin
Is calling love, hate.
The second greatest sin
Is calling servanthood, ambition.
The list need go no further.
There are no other sins of
    consequence.

IX

She felt the frost upon the grass
Where Slithe had stood
And was startled to see
A serpent lying in the frost,
His frozen coils sheathed in ice.
His Arctic being lured Regina powerfully.
She longed to touch the chilling specter
But recoiled from her longing.
Her intrigue seemed to beckon him
And he slithered close and large.
Trembling at his size she reached
To touch his frigid skin.
She lifted him, and he felt heavy
As the cold stones of Sanctuary.

"Kiss me," hissed the snake,
"And I will make you wise."

She grimaced at the thought
And yet she lifted up the serpent
Until his giant hooded head
Was opposite her face.
His hypnotic yellow eyes
Forbid her own to look away.
His neck fanned wide and cold.
His leathered face darted toward her own,
Until his gleaming fangs fell knife-like on her face.
In the flash of pain,
She dropped the hideous creature
And running terrified to Regis, clung to him.

Regis saw the double marks
Where tiny drops of venom hung with blood.
"Are these the marks of broken trust
Upon your face?" he asked.

She started to reply,
But the swimming world left her
As the golden venom stirred a warm sensation
And exhilarating dreams were born.
In her light mind she left her leaden body
And lifted upward,
Until she left the forest far below.
In her wild delirium she saw that
Slithe rose too, a serpent floating
Idly, oddly, in the air.

Regina touched the marks upon her face,
Thrilling at the ecstasy of flight
Above her lofty view of Sanctuary,
She flew and marveled at her power.

The flying Serpent, soaring at her side,
Shouted through the high, thin air,
"All this I'll give you, If
You will call love, hate."

Swimming through her fantasies
She wept in dreaming echoes.
"Oh, give me flight and sight."

"Come," cried the flying cobra-thing,
They settled earthward from their odyssey
And glided to a grassy knoll of waiting splendor.
There, a mound of diamonds
Beckoned her as gleaming need
Cold as the crystal ice
That she had seen upon the grass
Where the serpent's sting had
Made her drunk with dreams.
She reached to scoop a handful
Of the crystalline fascination,
And then . . . the gems were gone—evaporated
        into air.

"Ah . . . ah! Diamonds have their price,"
Slithe taunted.
"These, my queen, are only yours
If you will call love, hate."

Again she didn't answer him.
Her dream was suddenly alive
With glorious music.

"Riches are no prize,
Only he who gives them." The reptile scoffed.
She watched him change.
He elongated and thickened
Into a handsome man.
The venom coursing through her soul
Crowned rich her fantasies with a strong and
        powerful longing.
Slithe, now handsome, clothed with glory, called
        aloud.
"O come, Regina, run with me,
The heathered meadows beckon."
Inwardly she barely could resist.

He called temptingly again, "Give me all that
        you give
Your mere, mortal mate.
And you shall know true knowledge.
I'll endow you with such ecstasy
As will open wide the gates of understanding.
We both shall know . . . be free . . .
Oh, call love, hate, and live!"

"Be gone, deceiver!" She called out,
Struggling through the sluggish stupor
Of her fading dream.

She shook herself
And woke in Regis' arms.

And there, leaning against him,
She sobbed that she had trusted hate
And felt ashamed that she had passed so near to folly,
"Regis, my heart draws close to treachery.
I reach for all I hate
And hate myself for reaching.

"Why do I sometimes crave
The taste of all I must not eat?
My mind is damned by needs
I am ashamed to name.
I can drive Him from Sanctuary
Any time I wish,
And yet I keep him near, wishing . . . longing . . .
Reaching for apocalypse,
And dying . . . Oh, keep me from desire.
Teach me to rebuke all treachery with reason!"

Regis interrupted her,
"Worship, Regina, will heal
Your dread caprice,
And teach you life in responsibility.
Worship and let love
Put lust away."

"Then come at once," she urged,
"Back to the grotto altar and let us
Cry out 'love and Father'
Till lust shall lose its place
To adoration!
Oh, Father-Spirit, hold my unsure hand
And bid me trust what I can't understand!"

Hate is absolute zero:
The state where all moisture
    crystallizes
And every structure explodes with
    cold.
There, all romance is but a winter's
    tale.
And dreams grow porcelain with hate
Till love shatters, along with lovers
Who thought love's warmth
Could bid the ice repent
And save its frozen soul.

X

There's frost in Sanctuary!"
The Father-Spirit turned his head away in grief.
Regis and Regina were dumbfounded,
To know Earthmaker cried.

"You cry because of frost?"
Prince Regis asked.

"I weep because you willed
The coming of My enemy.
Notice how his recent presence
Spoils Sanctuary.
Where he stood the grass is dead—
The air too cold for any possibility of life.
Were he to have the scepter he desires
The world itself would die.
Evil lives in Sanctuary at your summons.
See his arctic scar on this good place.
Have you satisfied your longing?
Laid your appetites to rest?
Or, will you seek My enemy again
Till all this garden lies in ruin?
Can you now see how his hate
Can canker entire galaxies,
And spread contagions that infect the very stars."

An awful silence came.

The man and woman, downcast
In their shame, at length
Raised both their heads and pledged,
"Father,
Never shall we will
The death of love."

The Father-Spirit loved them.
"There is only one real power
That you should long to own: Self-denial!
Spend all you have to purchase it.
Lust after chains of servanthood—never thrones
    of pride.
For servants, worn by willful drudgery,
At last wear diadems.
Bridle all desire: For having what you want,
Will leave you groveling in wantonness.
Feed yourselves with hunger,
Then savor all you slowly eat.
Thus, self-denial will give you richness but
  keep you from excess.
Use this world, do not consume it.
Never pursue pleasure, rather let it find you . . .
At the end of every day . . .
Where you made discipline your friend.
For pleasure never comes in what you hold,
But in what holds on to you—compelling you
    to care.
Should life call you to be a martyr,
Do not despair
For those who would die for great reasons,
Also find great reasons for their living.
Think not that gaudiness is beauty
But simple ornament
Which lives only to reflect the light around it.
Turn from all desire to have,
Lest what you seek to own,
At last owns you!
Make no hour heavy with doubled greed
Rather let a giving spirit make you rich with
    sleek humility
That runs through troubled times.
Grow rich by giving up your purse.
Lay by your mace and rule.

Release your grasp and in your open hand
You'll find the world.
Die and greet the life-force
Created by your willful death.
For self-denial does empower the soul,
And those who hold their need to rule at bay,
Are kings and queens with empires in their sway."

Why do we long to touch
What we most fear?
Who can deny the cobra, deadly
    grace?
The luring symmetry of fanged face,
Yet if, spellbound, we reach
Into the serpent's place
Our life dissolves in venom with no
    trace.

XI

I could wish," sighed Regis,
"That there was something
Not quite human, not quite God.
Something knowing love
Yet touching hate."

The serpent suddenly was there.
Regis and Regina watched entranced as
The creature raised its glorious head
Into the morning sun.
Soon the Reptile eyes
Grew warm with life,
He spoke wistfully—like a king—
All recently deposed.
"Slithe I am now, but once
My name was Night Star.
I was and am and shall be
Brother to the light and to the dark.
I love all truth.
For I know the heart of falsehood
Is but integrity grown reasonable.
Good and bad are never values locked in stone,
They are only ways of seeing.

"To obey or disobey, is but artifice.
And nothing ever shall be right or wrong
Within itself.
If He who made you
Wags His finger in your face
Telling you love the good and fear the evil,
Remind Him you live free
Of all moral rigidity.
There is right that's only nearly right
And wrong that's not so wrong
And a lie that saves is better than destructive truth.

"And where's the trespass in a kind transgression?
Make your conscience judge
And you can purge the world of sin
And all the gods and devils will perish
With their good and evil categories.
Your Father lied to you.
There is no sin, till you define it so.
Sin is but the name of misery
That gods prescribe to make poor mortals fear
And teach them guilt.
What He calls 'sin' you've only to reverse and
Call it good.
Rename His old taboos,
And save your self from His confining moralisms.
You are guiltless when you say so,
Sin cannot live one second after *you* proclaim
        it dead!
Stroke my skin
And feel the innocence
We three shall share.
Let's take ourselves to bed."

"No! He warned us that intimacy can never be
        for three,"
Regis grew firm in his refusal.

"It is wrong? Sin, even?" Slithe scoffed.

"It is!" The Prince of Sanctuary
Now stood straight in his resolve.

"Wrong . . . Why? Is your nest too small?
Always wrong . . . evermore . . .
        eternity-without-end wrong?
Sometimes three can make the conversation ready,
The laughter frequent.
Think, man, and transform wrong to right.

Three is two grown generous.
My presence in the bower says that you both know
      hospitality
And kindness!
Since when is it a wicked deed to make space for
     a friend?"

And so that night the trio slept
Between the trees,
And when the morning came
Two humans and a snake
Woke in a common nest.
"Now see," Slithe said,
"We have done nothing wrong!
We spent the night as three
And yet we call it chastity!
Love's bed is big enough for all
Made broad by gracious minds."
He, slithering away, was swallowed up in dewy grass.
But the man and woman suddenly
Recalled Earthmaker's wondrous gift
Lamenting,
"Love for three can know no intimacy,
It spends it purse on grand obscenity."

Beware of mirrors
They lead us not to see ourselves
  But love ourselves
  Like poor Narcissus,
Who, grasping at his image died.
They say that floating in the
Water just above his
Wide-eyed, silent face
There was a butterfly.
Had he let it lead him into wonder,
He might have loved science, not
    himself,
And lived to cure the world of plague.

XII

The morning found Earthmaker
And His children
At the base of the two trees.

"Behold, the morning tree," the Father-Spirit said.
"At this tree's base is spade and hoe.
These tools invite you to deny mere ease
So the work to which you give yourselves
Can make your understanding grow."

Regis grabbed the spade
And turned the earth
Until his untried hands, wood-wounded,
Bled and blisters stung his fingers.
When he had stopped to rest
Regina spied two objects underneath the sunset tree.

She ran to them and Regis followed.
A crown and mirror leaning up against the bark
Allured her.

Regis and Earthmaker watched Regina
Place the crown upon her head,
And gaze into the mirror.
She was indeed a queen,
A Maya over paradise—
Beautiful and regal.

"Be not deceived, Regina," Earthmaker cried.
"Mirrors chain us to our vanity.
Serve and be free.
Leave off empty admiration and come to self-denial.
Cling to these tools!
Servanthood is better than acclaim.
The shovel breaks the hand in time,
But it is richer than this false crown.

Learn to spend yourself in work,
For though it cut the hands,
It dares to dream of changing
Desert into Paradise.
Work wears honor and
Shames all fruitless indolence.
Calloused hands made crowns look tinsel.
Work is pride.

"Work is glory.
Work is sweat in harvest fields—
The royal right to ask for bread.
Work teaches sleep to slumber, undisturbed,
And scorns to beg or steal.
Work alone understands the Sabbath truth
That six days of labor wakes the seventh day
    with honor.
And they who earn an honest Sabbath
Can worship Me, cleansing their fatigue."

Earthmaker walked to the mirror
And swung the golden circlet
Through the gleaming glass,
Shattering the image of a naked empress.
When the crown had melted into nothingness
The Father reached out to her.
"Your enemy has placed these objects here
To lure you into self-importance.
My little one, bridle your vanity—
Make self-denial the scepter of humility."
Earthmaker handed him the spade and her the hoe.
"Mirrors sometimes lead to false esteem
But spade and worship wash the desert green."

Unbridled lust:
A cannibal committing suicide
By nibbling on himself.

XIII

Regina woke before her mate
And saw the serpent rising
From the waters of the pool.

"Before your man awakes," the reptile hissed,
"Come with me, and I shall teach you choosing."

"Would I, who prize my husband's love,
Make any choice beyond his free consent?"

"Come not to choose,
But to consider choice.
Make yourself wise, then choose."
As she shrank away, he grinned,
"Do you recoil because you fear me?
Is my form strange to you?
Consider how much alike we really are."

He changed himself once more into a man,
Whose charm invited ease
And so she rose,
And looking down upon the sleeping form
Of her beloved, doubted.
She turned to Slithe.
Her doubts ebbed.
Suddenly she wanted something more . . .
A cleansing from the boredom of the hoe and
        spade.

"Should I worship?" she asked, half aloud.
"Yes," said the handsome tempter,
"But not Him who comes as wind!
Worship this," he said,
Gesturing to his powerful frame.
"And this," he said pointing to her body.

"Let us worship *us*, and knowledge will be ours.
Did you find the mirror and the crown I left at
    sunset?"

"I did, but they are gone now!"

"Gone . . . why gone?"

"My Father told me that to admire myself was most
    ignoble."

"Why? Did He not create you perfectly?
Surely beauty has some right to celebrate itself.
Before He woke you from the birthing altar,
He gazed as spirit-artist on what He had created,
Knowing you were the fitting finale
Of all that He had made.
Now He denies you mirrors?
When He admires you, it is mere artistry,
And yet when you admire yourself
It is evil vanity?"
He motioned unto her,
"Follow me."

She did.
They walked till they had
Left the bower far behind.
He took her hand.
His flesh felt cold.
She drew away.
And yet he would not let
Her hand escape his grasp.
"You are a goddess, beautiful.
Shout it without shame.
Vanity does not exist.
Like sin, it's missing from the healthy mind.
Your beauty calls to me,

And summons me to celebrate
What you must learn to celebrate: yourself!
I love you.
I worship you!
We shall do what we will.
The world is free of sin
For we decree it so!
Vanity begone!
Your beauty is an icon for us both."

They stopped. He faced her
Then he drew her close,
And holding her in an embrace
He whispered love
As bargains of betrayal.
"Fruit have I," he said,
"Whose life-red sap
Will teach your blood to sing."
His face moved toward her own
Till it filled all her vision,
And then he whispered,
"Regina, let your freedom flow as choice,
Kiss this bearded face, and hate will be for you
A glory warm as dust.
Feed hunger and embrace this craving night.
Let love grow generous with appetite."

A solitary soldier believed himself a
        regiment
And so he died, as he saw it,
A whole army felled with a single ball.
Fools are made secure by egotism
But the wise, knowing all their
        weaknesses,
Gather into troops
To walk through Dante's mind.

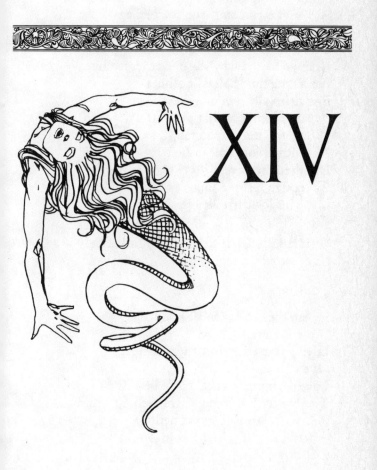

XIV

She tore herself away
Yet did not run . . . Slithe beckoned
And walked on.
Gradually she turned
And followed comfortably behind
At last at closer step, she reached again
To take his hand.
This time she found him altogether pleasant
And wondered why she'd ever feared him.
For a long time he said nothing.
She also walked in quietness.
At last, arriving at that place
Where the trees stood tall,
As sentinels of choice, she sat.
He stood, however,
As though his standing
Made his logic irresistible.

"Is it hard to learn to hate?" She asked.
"How would it set me free?"

"Hate comes easily,"
He smirked at her small knowing.
"Love it is that's difficult.
Love sets itself against the principle,
Of death and all defeat.
Love promises a world made beautiful
Then struggles to transform each ugly thing.
And in its struggle grows neurotic,
Always dreaming better things
Insisting upon excellence.
And excellence—demands, demands!
Never satisfied, and drives us
To compete with yesterday
And leaves us weeping that today
Is ever so much less than we had planned."

"Fair woman, I admire you
For abandoning your husband to look for love
Outside of your tight, cozy nest of mutual
      enslavement.
See how free you have become, away from Regis.
But you are still too much the slave of
Earthmaker's narrow requirements."

"Why should I hate? Why?
What in that bitter passion is divine?"

"Taste and see!
Come to knowledge and be free
Leave your humanness!
Be what you are: a goddess!
Close your eyes, Regina,
And see the glory that can be,
When you have the courage
To reach out for it."

She closed her eyes and in the darkness
Created by the simple act,
Slithe made her see a wondrous self.
She fell upon the warm red earth.
She lengthened in exhilaration
Till she was cobra-formed like Slithe.
They crawled as fast as eagles flew
And laughed in lusty sunlight.
They wound around the tree of choice
And climbed with coils of power
Till finally, high as serpents vie,
As cobras lying on the sky,
They reached the sun-red fruit.
"Give me, give me!" cried Regina,
Reaching fangward in the blue.

Regina's coiled form gave suddenly away.
She fell

And in her falling wept,
And hit the crusted earth
Then her awareness faded and was gone.

When her soaring reveries were dead,
She was alone and gasped to see
She held the blood-red fruit of choice.
Its shiny rind was still unbroken.
She knew she had not eaten.
She cast the fruit as far she might throw it
And hurried off to find the Prince of Sanctuary.
Behind her, low in gloating dust
The slit-eyed Slithe
Slithered on the pathway after her.
So evil always slithers after good
Drawing us with lust from "is" to "should."

Hate is born
When men call evil good.
And like an infant serpent
Bursting from its
Small, confining shell,
It never can be
Cased so small again.

XV

Earthmaker came at first light
Speaking directly to Regina.
"You've been with him?"

"I have,
For he draws me with such power
I feel that I must follow."

"Is he instructing you in hate?"
The Father-Spirit asked.

"He tries, but I'm committed unto love."

"Make sure your pledge,
Lest you in but a single taste
Devour your destiny.
Beware of compromise.
You play these days
Along the precipice
Of utter loss.
You've toyed so often now
with desperate caprice.
Indeed you've gone so far
You have only now to look on truth
And name it falsehood."

"I never shall!" the woman said.
But her speech fell slow
As if her promise lacked assurance,
Even to herself.
The forest sun fell in a compelling mood
Which leaked dividing shafts of light
Through all the leafy ceiling.
One of those rich rays
Fell upon the coils of
The fanged deceiver.

The snake lifting up his head,
Shouted at Earthmaker.
"Set her free!
Are You afraid
That given choice
She might choose wide enough
To be gods like You and me?
Regina, let not His Fatherhood
Call your bondage 'Daughter'!
Renounce Him!
He was my master only once.
Now I am free
Because of courage.
Your Father is afraid
That you, like me, will leave Him
And He will find Himself
Once more alone within the universe
He says He owns.
He sees—Don't you, Earthmaker?—
That you and Regis daily grow more hungry,
For all that He calls treachery
And I call utter liberty.
He hears already
How, the distant music comes."

"What music?" asked the woman.

"The music of denial.
The music of betrayal
Which will fill his private symphony
With raucous discord—
And bring at last true
Music to your life."
The serpent laughed
And slithered deep in shadows.

The woman turned imploringly,
"Father,

Must we ever live with him?
Take him from our sanctuary!"

"I did not bring him here.
I will not take him hence.
He came here at your will.
He will go of his accord
When you desire him gone.
Quit titillating all your appetites,
And Sanctuary will be free of him."

"But we have never asked him in this place,"
Regis spoke denial.

"Not in words, perhaps.
But what you harbor in your hearts,
Your tongues would scorn to speak aloud."

"Has the World-Hater always found
His joy in hate?" She asked.

"Hardly!" The Father-Spirit said.
"He was made to serve in love
But within him began to grow
The desire to have My place
And rule the stars on thrones
More lofty than My own.
He soon despised My realm and me.
Once he had cursed My love, he laughed at every
     dignity.
He plans the same cruel violence for you."

"Father," cried the man,
"Were we to choose the path of hate . . .
Would You still love us?"

"I would. I can do no other,
For love's the substance of My being.

But should you choose to call hate, love,
Ice like that which kills the grass
Around the World-Hater's feet
Would crush the glory of this glen
In icy tonnage, mauling Sanctuary.

"Consider the beauty of this realm and bid
Your appetites remember consequence.
Garrison your hearts.
Say no to all destructive lust:
Obey it and the blood of unbegotten empires
Will swallow Terra up in pointlessness,
A darksome world in search of self.
Which flies through night without identity
And wonders why she ever came to be."

The moth that trusts the candle's fire
Is willing martyr to her own desire.

XVI

With new resolve
The man and woman steeled themselves
Against all contemplation of disobedience.
They did not swear that they would never hate.
They, rather, lived rehearsing love.

So full was love's rehearsal
That when dawn awoke the pair
The Serpent was not there.
They found this no surprise,
For their thoughts were lost in adoration.

"Regina, morning wakes my heart," Regis spoke low,
"Daily now I try to measure
What I cannot measure, love! I love you,
With a love which leaps its high-walled doubts,
And lives to touch your face
And look into your eyes
Born like diamonds in the starlight.
Kiss me, and let your kiss be the pledge
That I will always hold you here,
Not just enriching Sanctuary
But making my life possible.
For without your love, I die—
As song, strangled into silence,
Or reason smothered by loneliness."

The morning found them wandering—
Walking, stopping to embrace,
Kissing first in shadows and then in sunlight.
For reasons only lovers understand,
She wove a chain of Hyacinth
And draped the lei
Across his chest and kissed him.
Then like a forest vixen

She exploded to a run
Teasing him with chase.
He pursued!
He caught her in the glade.
They fell laughing in the russet meadow.

"No life but this—forever," he shouted to the sky.
And they laid together,
Quiet in the splendor of soft breezes
And the warming of the sun.
"Today," he said, "Let's go to see the gates.
And celebrate ourselves
As we behold the barrenness
Of life beyond His care.
Perhaps in seeing this great emptiness
We'll find all sense rebuked
And know insanity for what it is:
Choosing any opposite of love."

They walked in silence through the day
Until at last they saw ahead of them
The gates of Sanctuary.
In hesitance at last,
They climbed the minarets
Which held the hinges
Of the lofty portals.

Far below them stretched the desert.
Where death rose up in dunes,
That seemed the burial mounds
Of civilizations still unborn.
Behind them Sanctuary rose
In lapis waterfalls, lavishly froth-dancing in cascades.

"Pray we shall never have
To live out there," the woman said,
Pointing sand-ward.

"Oh, Father," Regis prayed.
"May all You are, suffice us."

"Hold me," she pled suddenly startled.
He did but felt her trembling with old fears.
Something evil had
Brushed past her feet.

"Whatever is it?" he cried.

"Look," she pointed to the serpent
Now slithering to the highest ramparts
Of the northern spire.
There its circled shape
Left off its reptile form,
Rose, wavered, and
Untwisted into a man.

"Why is he here?" Regis asked her.
"Could you have desired his coming
In the face of this dead, desolate
Expanse of wasteland?"

"No," she cried.
"I never did desire his coming . . . I . . ."
Silence.
"Yes," she admitted at last.
"I . . . I only wondered
What it must be like
To walk in sand
When we have walked so long in paradise.
I only wondered if the desert . . ."

Her speech was interrupted
By the laughter
Of the World-Hater.

He stopped his mockery, shouting,
"This . . . not this . . . shall be your home."
His arm swept from the forest to the desert.
"You shall break these gates with courage
And live without these walls."

Considering his prophecy
And the desert out before them,
Regis shouted to his face:
"Go, Slithe, we are committed unto trust
We shall worship, with all loyalty,
Him who woke us unto life.
At the edge of emptiness we raise His name,
And celebrate the clay from which we came!"

Ego plays at life
To fill the hours with smiling politics
But only power can satisfy the
    arrogant.

XVII

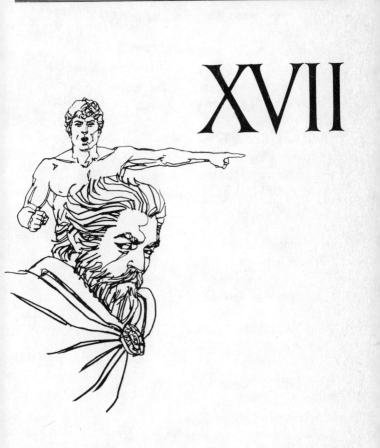

As they turned their backs
Upon the desert and started to descend,
Regina asked Regis,
"If the Father-Spirit rules the universe
Where is our dominion?"

"What need have we to rule?"

"I only wondered if all this land outside
Could be ours.
Could we own it, as he owns us?"

"What's there to own . . . but wasteland,
Shifting sands and howling winds?"

"Still, wouldn't it be better
To own a kingdom dry and dead
And have some throne, at least?
If we owned it as he owns this,
We'd both be Kings."

In the moment of her final sentence
Slithe reappeared smiling.
"There's a world out there
And room enough for all to rule.
You need but speak the word!
Then you will be like Earthmaker,
With power and scepter."

"But, Slithe, did you not once believe
That you could rule
In His expanded universe?
See what a wreck your own betrayal
Made of such assumptions."
Regis gestured toward the arid realm.

"But see," the World-Hater said,
"I can enter the world beyond these gates
As freely as I have entered Sanctuary.
You cannot.
You choose not to be king out there
And here you never can be king.
For here within these gates
He alone holds power.
The sand is empire waiting to be claimed.
Come rule! Know, and be gods."

"Leave us, Prince of Evil," cried Regis,
"You took the Diadem of Holy Love
Defiling it with pride.
Can you now claim to teach us virtue,
While your vile hypocrisy still hungers
To spread the wasteland of your banishment
Inside these walls of grace?
I have found you out,
PRETENDER! FRAUD! AND LIAR!
Life knows no more debauching infamy,
Than that which answers love with treachery."

"If you are the Son of God make this
    stone bread."
"I will indeed," the false messiah said.
"And from this stone nearby, I shall
    make wine."
Thus greed can fill a glutton's plate
And utter selfishness may dine.

XVIII

Will the Father-Spirit
Really drive us from this place?
If He has so much power
Could He not pinch some little corner
From His Kingdom and offer it to us?"

"Please Regina . . . careful . . . lest you call
          love hate.
Let's go once more
To the grotto altar and bow in adoration.
Let us whisper 'Love' and 'Father'
And adore the Spirit that enfranchised
Our once-dead clay with Life."

"No . . . husband . . . go alone.
I've lost my taste for worship now.
I need to be alone to think."
She walked away in ponderous melancholy.

Regis also walked alone in heaviness.
He wondered just how often in these latter days,
His woman talked with Slithe.

He passed a lionness and lion
And remembered how alone he once had felt.
Love was somehow dying,
And even as he clung to it
It sifted, sand-like, through his longing fingers.
He recalled old joys—
New love, touching as first splendor.
His mind was camera to hurried scenes
Of laughing lovers running in the sun.
A sudden, scalding grief made his body shudder.

He wandered, as though the night
Refused him anything

But grieving darkness.
At length his aimless feet came across an old path
That he and his now doubtful queen
Had often walked together.
A chilling fear seized him
As he saw the naked footprints
Of his beloved
Wandering in soft earth.
For there the small depressions
Of her feet
Mingled with the curious, soft,
Embossing serpent trails.
He pondered those strange trails
And asked himself how long
Could Sanctuary live.
These days were hurtling to ruin
As though their eager pace—
Made furious by every dread he felt—
Could barely wait to stab at Fatherhood.
Life in the bosom of great love, was ebbing.
Life as he had known it, dreamed it, clung to it
Was dying.

His tears fell in the dust,
Making visible coagulations of his grief
Among the slithering indentations,
Of a serpent's belly
And the footprints of his own beloved,
        thoughtless queen.
He cried aloud, stretching his entreaty
Toward the heavens—
Grasping nothing in his closing fingers:
"Choose wisely, Queen, remembering the cost
Lest love and sanctuary both be lost!"

A beggar asked a millionaire,
"How many more dollars
Would it take to
Make you truly happy?"
The millionaire,
Reaching his gnarled hands
Into the beggar's cup, replied,
"Only one more!"

XIX

When the sun was high
Regis found Regina piling fruit
From the morning tree.
She stacked it feverishly
With nervous hands
That flew about their task.
Her eyes were crazed
By some wild drivenness.
When the stack seemed
About to tumble,
Regis, reached out asking, "Why?"

"So there will be enough for tomorrow."

"There has always been enough.
Abundance, here, is great as love.
It always comes with sunrise.
Have His blessings ever failed us?
Have we ever woke in Sanctuary
With too few evidences of His care?
See, already, what a waste
Your greed has made.
The fruit at the bottom of your pile
Begins to darken.
On the tree it would have been connected
To the source of life
And lived until we needed it.
What sudden spirit in you
Stores this rotting fruit
Against your insecurity?
Has the serpent led you even more
Into his web of doubt?"

"Regis! I will not have you slur the Serpent!
He is friend, mentor, healer unto me.
He makes me doubt only that

Which should be doubted.
He said that life
Can interrupt itself with pain.
See this scar?"
She held her wrist to him.
"I got it picking berries
When a tiny limb
Thrust its knife-like branch
Into my hand.
But when the serpent came
I felt much better."

"Then why this dying pile of fruit?"

"Because Slithe says that life is fragile . . .
Think, Regis! Open up your eyes!
The Serpent's words may save us!
If we should have to live
Beyond the gates
We could carry all this fruit
Into the fruitless desert
And there we still might live."

"Regina!" Regis was surprised
To find himself so near to shouting.
"There is no life beyond the gates!
There is no love beyond the gates!
There is no walk with
Our beloved Father there!"

"Slithe says the sand is warm in sunshine.
He claims there is no foliage there
To block the stars at night.
And that the desert sun rises clear
Unobstructed by the forest.
He counsels us that it is better to be free
In glorious sand than to be chained
In Paradise by love.

He says there is a certain thrill
In disobedience that we have never known . . .
That ecstasy more often comes,
Not in what is right
But in what is nearly right—
And great exhilaration comes
In what is clearly wrong.
O, Regis, why can we not trust him . . .
At least a little?
We trust the Father-Spirit.
The Hater says that we have grown—
Too stingy in our trust.
That life is broader
Than the narrow cell that
We have built ourselves
From his confining love."
She paused a moment . . .
"Oh, I am learning much from Slithe!"

The man stood silent.
He looked again
At the dying pile of fruit and said to her,
"When will you have enough
In this decaying pile
To make you feel content?"

"I just need a little more."
She turned and picked another piece
And laid it on the pile.
She walked away, hurried,
As though she had
Some frenzied business to attend.
He watched her till she passed
A sunlit section of the path
And then he saw her pick up something
And hold it to the sky.
She was holding up the serpent,
Swirling him in golden ecstasy.

Tears flooded Regis' sight,
Washing his despair into a blur,
Till in the distant circle of the sun,
The snake changed to a man,
Who then lifted Sanctuary's queen
And held her up, exulting.
Their playful laughter,
Stabbed Regis
With a killing numbness.
He stumbled to his knees
Burying his torn face in his hands
While they hurried on into the depth of green
And their laughter died away.

Regis wept!
The fruit that now lay dying on the ground
Was too obscene to hold his interest.
Disconsolate, he made his way
To that warm place
They once had called their nest.
There the sun came slow and late,
And the sapphire pool
Colored early afternoons.
He sat, in thought,
Reflecting by the water
For quite some time
Before he noticed
An odd collection of leaves
Knit together in a strange fashion.
When he picked the leafy object up
It appeared a crude kind of garment . . .
Like the one the Hater wore, only shabby.
He knew his woman had fashioned it,
So that she could be like . . .
He stopped his mind,
"Come, O Father-Spirit, and draw near.
Rebuke these doubts which circle me with fear."

The illicit
Does not exhilarate.
It but indicts:
The sweetness of all adultery
Leaves just before the splendor,
Destroying the ecstasy
We thought might linger
To eliminate the shame.

XX

This is the place of choice!"
Slithe encircled her and asked,
"Are you afraid?"

"And what is fear?" She laughed.
"The choice of timid men
Who live in bondage.
Have I told you of the joy
I feel with you?
So long I have obeyed
The strict confinement
Of the Father-Spirit's world.
Now I shall declare
That I am free . . .
Free and I will choose at last,
Even as a goddess.
I shall live in Sanctuary
Or wherever I shall choose.
But I shall choose."

Slithe slipped into his other form.
His handsome body dwindled, shrinking
Until his serpentine remains
Curled at her feet on the brilliant turquoise
Floor of Sanctuary.
He then twisted around her legs
And rose in circling coils
About her naked body.
At last she took him from her upper bosom
And gazed into his slitted eyes.
His mouth broke open
And his fangs dropped gleaming white
Into the sun.

"You can't frighten me," she laughed once more.
"Today is my day to be free of fear.

Today . . . I choose . . . I make my own way."
She set the serpent on the ground
And felt exhilarated—like a queen—
Queen Regina, sceptered by her daring.
She ruled and watched her serpent king,
And smiled in giddiness,
Naïveté crowned by adolescent vanity.

As his simple queen looked on,
Slithe slithered to the tree of choice,
The tree of freedom . . .
The tree of knowledge . . .
The tree of living where she would.
The tree that promised
All the warmth of desert sand
And sunrise brilliantly inflamed.

She watched, mesmerized
As Slithe picked fruit
By nipping stems
With gleaming teeth.
One piece fell,
And it settled ever downward
In a floating fashion.
But before it hit the ground
Slithe, himself, was somehow there.
He caught it as it dawdled earthward
And extended her the fruit.

"Eat and take it to the man!"

"He will not eat!"

"He will!" The World-Hater cried,
"For what I could not achieve with him
You will.
For he will not permit in you
What he does not find within himself.

You see, I am content to be alone.
And so for that matter is your Father-Spirit.
But you and the man need company.
It will be no time at all before
He feels again the same, old killing loneliness
That once made life unbearable.
He will eat, dear Regina, he will eat."

"But let us not spoil this moment."
He led her to a shaded portion
Of the grove.
They leaned back against a tree.
He embraced her as she lifted
Life's denial to her lips.
She ate, and in the glory of the taste
Her world shook beneath her.
The stars spun above.
Vision blurred
And the green of Sanctuary shouted
Hues of wild and waxen glory.
Her whole body seemed alive, afire,
Shot through with
Passing currents of night storms
Electrified with forked glory.

But in a moment the ecstasy was gone.
She stood alone . . . And naked . . .
Odd, now she knew both words at once
And yet to be both "alone" and "naked"
Were heavy terms of judgment.
When shame arrives
We somehow must have company.
And so the naked queen clutched both fruit and
        shame
And hurried off
To seek a reinstatement
Of lost innocence.
Her face—no, all her being—

Was flushed with hot despair.
Tears tracked like crackling porcelain
Yet cut like molten stone into her faithless
    stammering.
"My treachery lies as burning disobedience.
My foolish ecstasy was but
The ash of momentary fire.
Oh, Regis, please forgive my wretched sin.
Your love alone can make me clean again!"

The wings of demons are as white as
    angels' wings
Their halos are as golden bright
They sing as well as angels, too
But only when it's night.

XXI

Regis came upon Regina holding
To the half-eaten fruit.
She was singing softly to herself,
Unaware that in the leafy walls
Of a now alien forest
Her beloved heard her song.
Here and there her broken soul
Ruptured her lament and choked the music of
Her requiem for love.

"A flash of pleasure have I bought with pain—
A tiny moment's hurried ecstasy.
And I have sullied love with stain
And answered faith with treachery.
Once both our world and love were shining new.
Then we took pleasure in the golden leas
And laughed as lovers laugh—all noble, true—
And felt the thrill of honest ecstasy.
But here I hold the witness in my hand,
The sticky sweet of all my appetite.
My craven lust to call rank evil, grand—
The queen of sun, gone whoring after night.
I wore the crown of Terra, and I owned
The portion of a queen. I loved a king
Whose gentle arms forbade me walk alone.
Whose husky voice made Sanctuary sing.
Our palace was of beams left whole inside
The trees. And stones unquarried were the tower.
The wife of Regis soon became the bride
Of greed, the mistress of the dog of power.
O Regis, kiss our love in requiem,
Lament the queen who laid her scepter by.
Who cast off sense, called pleasure whim,
And taught the sanctuary sun to cry.
Forgive your soiled queen her soiled crown.
Who saw love everywhere, yet reached for lust.

Who pulled her sky-born king to naked ground
And chained her sky-barred eagle in the dust."

The music ended,
Regina turned toward the trees
Where Regis waited
And in an instant
Each saw the other.

"Regis . . . Regis . . . King!" the woman cried,
She ran to him,
"Hold me, so I will
No longer be alone."

"But you've never been alone!"
He said as he embraced her.
"You're trembling," he said.
He was devastated to find her
Innocence so scarred,
To see her
So encased in moods of fear
That he had never known.

"I'm so afraid!" she blurted
Clinging closer than she ever had.

"Alone, afraid?
I heard your Requiem . . .
You've tasted the forbidden?"

"Oh . . . I have eaten . . . Eaten!
I have known such ecstasy
As you cannot imagine.
I felt the glory of this place . . .
Of nakedness . . . and . . ."

"And only now do you know nakedness . . .
Have your deeds

Undressed your heart?
Do you love me, Regina?"

"Yes, yes! I love all but him.
Him I hate . . . Slithe!
The World-Hater!
Do you not hate him too?'

"I do not hate at all . . .
Nor am I lonely or afraid . . ."

"Eat with me," she begged,
Pulling the piece of fruit
From behind her back.
"Leave me not alone.
Don't you see our world is now divided
Into fourths?
There is the hater,
Your Father-Spirit . . ."

"He used to be *your* Father-Spirit too,"
He cried in interruption.

"Fourths . . ."
She put his speech aside . . .
"Yes . . . Fourths . . . Your Father-Spirit,
The Hater . . . my lonely self and you.
For you, too, are alone.
You are as alone in your faithfulness
As I am in my deceit.
I cannot stand this wall between us."

"Deliver me . . . please love me
More than Him who gave us Sanctuary
And then each other.
I know He'll come
And drive me from this place.
I cannot face the desert by myself.

Please, eat!"
He watched her piteous pleading
As his mind recalled her little pile
Of dying fruit and realized
The Hater had bade her trust a lie.

Regis turned from her and walked away.
His heart was crushed by her entreaty
And the love he held for Earthmaker.
He knew he could not please them both.
His agony no longer sought
To make a choice of living free or captive.
His was the necessity of choosing
When every choice was wrong.

If he ate not
She'd die alone in bleakness.
And if he ate he'd crush the heart of his Creator.
He paused beside the sapphire pool, looking down.
He studied his tired face.
It cracked in pain and fell away.
"My wife, my Father: Which shall I choose?
Oh, Father,
If I should try to tell the fullness of all meaning,
The very reason I find existence dear,
The inwardness that makes me eager to awake,
They all should spell one word, 'FATHER!'
I swell when I behold Your coming in the rain,
I thrill to feel Your sunlight on my skin.
You are all in all to me.
I have been loved by love too powerful
To occupy any mortal form
Or try to case itself in anything,
That may be touched.
You meet me in my worship . . .
Caress me as wind . . . end all my loneliness,
And best of all You call me 'SON!'
Never has Your love awakened me,

But that I adore the light,
And speak love's holiest name, 'FATHER!'"

"But, O my beloved!"
He saw Regina in his mind and spoke to her,
"If, besides His love that gave me being,
I should be given just three syllables,
And then commanded never more to speak,
Those glorious syllables would be 'REGINA!'
And they would be enough to say
That when a man is touched
By love's full presence,
His life was worth the clay.

"Regina, you were my morning,
And the sun looking down on our relationship
Cursed his distance from this planet.
The stars at night
Saw themselves reflected in your eyes
And damned their lack of brilliance.
And when I kissed you in the fields,
I knew that life would give me ecstasy,
But for the asking.
And when the ecstasy arrived,
I measured splendor by the sky-fulls.
O Goddess, did I worship you too much?
Did I cherish you beyond the strength
I needed just to hold
To what my soul adored?
Now at last, this double love
That made me rich, steals everything.
And leaves me groveling in loveless poverty,
Where ardor lies, at last, in ashes.
Regina . . . queen! Earthmaker . . . Father!
O agony that is mine, to love both you and Him.
I cannot force my undeciding heart
To spurn my wife and take my Father's part."

"Bring me a long, warm coat."
"You must be freezing."
"No, just ashamed."

XXII

Regis wandered through the days.
From time to time he studied
Those huge trees that marked the place of choice.
He doted on Earthmaker's love,
And their delight before the woman came . . .
Before the serpent ever coiled in pristine sunlight
Infecting simple beauty with disease.

He thought about his great delight
When first the woman blessed his world.
He called to mind their walks,
The closeness of her warmth . . .
The sweet smell of her hair
When his chest
Was pillow to her head.
He thought of paradise . . .
Of Sanctuary and wished it wider.
And then in chilling inwardness
He thought of all the endless miles
Of stretching desert that lay beyond the walls,
And those high gates that sealed them in.
He shuddered to think that those same gates
Would shut out his beloved
And seal him in, alone, forever!

And then, could he expect the Father-Spirit
To fashion him a new, unspoiled love?
Could he start again with some new Regina
Made to end his aching loneliness once more?
But he wanted no "new" Regina—
Only she who first reigned over terra with himself.

Suddenly he froze.
He had not seen Regina
During the sojourn of his brokenness.
Might the Father-Spirit already have set her
Beyond the gates?
The question drove him in haste

To seek the bower again.
It was there that they had recently separated.
He called to her. She did not answer.
Certain now that
She must already be outside of Sanctuary,
He called to her again.
He ran in frenzied need but could not find her.
Weary with the agony of searching,
He fell asleep
And waited for the coming of the Father-Spirit.
He dreamed of his beloved wandering the desert,
Lamenting her treachery.

When he awoke he was gloriously aware
Of Regina's wondrous form
Nestled there beside him.
He felt her body shivering
Even as he drew her close.
Her pain was his pain now.
"Earthmaker will soon come and separate us.
You can no longer live in Sanctuary."

Suddenly he knew what he must do.
"Give me the fruit.
I'll eat.
We'll leave together."

"No, please!" she begged;
She'd clearly changed her mind.
"At first I wanted that, but I see more clearly
You've done nothing wrong.
He will not punish you for my sake.
Stay here and live.
Do not commit my folly."

"To live alone
Is not to live at all!" he cried.
"I once lived alone—Nevermore!
Give me the fruit!"

"I don't know where it is!" she lied.
Lying was easier for her now.
She was glad it was permitted.
For it seemed one simple lie
Would save her beloved
Even as it condemned her to exile.
But it was to little avail.
For even as she lied, he saw the truth:
The fruit lay beckoning like sunset.
For her the fruit was sweet at first taste.
For him all that remained was galling emptiness.
He grabbed at disobedience, choked at the sourness!
The sap was liquid fire
That spun a dream of futile reaching.
His Father walked away from him
As he reached out
And grasped the empty air.
"Loss . . . loss . . . loss . . ."

His dreaming cried—
The trees of Sanctuary withered.
The gates were closing him outside.
His Father turned with reaching
But his own weak stretching arms
Were far too short.
Then came the dark.
He groped in blindness in the desert
Crying as a child in the night.
"Father, Father, Father,
Forgive! Forgive! Forgive!"

He woke to find,
The crying of his dream was real.

They both sobbed now ashamed
Of all they had done.
And clinging to each other
In the face of coming night,
They waited for the dawn's first beckoning
To call their faithlessness to reckoning.

They say that dying often brings
A hurried cinema of all our lives.
In its spastic flashing reels is Adam
Trying hard to hold to oily Eden,
Weeping as it slips away.

XXIII

They came at last—old enemies—
Whose warring hostilities had fallen
On the battlefield of two weak human wills.

"Will you walk them to the gates,
Earthmaker, or shall I?"
The World-Hater mocked.
"Look," he laughed at their crude coverings.

The man and woman looked down
At the hastily appointed leafy shields
They had draped about themselves
In a vain attempt to hide from the piercing eyes
    of Him
Who looked through skin and so beheld their
    hearts.
They only stood in silence—
Wishing themselves smaller.
Begging inwardly that the distant mountains fall
    upon them.

"It is the end of dignity," the Hater gloated.
"See them now, Earthmaker, made little by their
    infidelity.
Now they hate—so far only me . . .
But soon, perhaps, each other.
And, oh, the glorious hate of all of their
    descendants,
That, in millennia to come, shall battle-bleed Your
    world!"

The Father-Spirit grieved.

The Hater gloated, "I once served at Your right hand
And knew Your promises!

It was too small a gift then—it is too small now.
These two have found that Your esteem
Was not the altar they desired . . .
They wanted what I wanted . . .
And what you never seem to share . . . *power!*"

"Power," the Father-Spirit murmured,
Only slightly louder than the brook
That splashed in white through Sanctuary.
"Power is only grandeur to him who wields it.
To those who languish underneath its crushing
    heel,
It destroys every shred of dignity."

A silence followed and the Hater hissed,
"Behold Your fallen royalty."
He gestured to the couple
Who listened, wounded at their conversation.
"Their nakedness is inward—
And yet they feel it outward.
Their fallenness delights me.
Homo Sapiens,
Man the knowing! Indeed!
Hah!
Homo Horribilis!
Alas, if knowing only made him good!
But see your lovers wrapped in shame!
Their children's children will
Lay waste each other
In a hundred thousand, pointless wars—
Each one based on hate.
Today, Earthmaker,
I close the garden of Your hopes.
Go ahead! Try to sell each coming generation
    peace!
They'll always come to me for apples!"
He sneered, then laughed,

Till his laughter leapt to howling!
When howling finally folded to a hiss
He dwindled earthward and slithered off.

"Come," the Father-Spirit beckoned, "Come . . ."

The man looked at his wife and said,
"We must leave now."

The three walked together for the last time
On the shaded paths they once enjoyed in hope,
When new laughter
Was the raucous joy
Announcing man had come.
Now a pall of silence shrouded them with pain.

The Father-Spirit spoke at last,
"There is coming to the world you will inherit
A Singer who will sing a song of dignity and life.
And Terra, in a happier age shall see Sanctuary
        born again."

"Beyond these gates
Life will be hard.
And worse, it will be temporary.
But remember my promise: a Singer,
That you may live without despairing."

They reached the towers
Which rose like monuments of exile,
To mystify the tiny pair
Now dwarfed by their betrayal.
The woman wept!
The man comforted her.
Slowly they moved past the minarets.
The gates stood open only for a moment,

Silhouetting them against the sand.
And Regis, reaching up to heaven cried—

"Hell is a lust for dark by those in light.
Our infamy has conquered day with night!"

The gates clanged shut—

Every baby comes as evidence
That God still dreams of Eden.
Sift Messianic mangers, and you'll
    find
Wherever Spirit and the flesh connect,
Wherever time and Ages intersect,
Some loving God lies in a human nest
And suckles milk at a Madonna's
    breast.

XXIV

The days were long
And marked by murderous work
For both of them,
And yet they always longed
To see each other
In the first light of morning.

"I love you," said Regina, now grown older.
"And today when the stones cut your hands
And the ground
Resists your efforts to bring life,
Remember this—I love you."

He looked at her hair,
Already streaked with gray
And knew in time
Their eyes would no longer hold the light,
Nor view the mountains they had grown to love.

"The years steal life.
I shall not always be here
Nor shall these eyes forever gaze
Upon the face for which I traded immortality."

"There is something I must tell you," said the
        woman.
"It will make your time in the fields much shorter.
I am with child—
A child, who like ourselves, may make the wrong
        choices
But here and there he may choose right.
And we, as our Father-Spirit promised,
Will have a chance
To start again
With life in innocence."

He embraced her
It seemed a sign.

And so the planet Terra came to be.
It circled through wide fields of stars
And waited, and in the waiting
Lay the glory of a promise
Living side by side with pain.
In time the hurt would die
For a promise always outlives pain.

Time watched the exiled king and queen
Till in the autumn of their lives
They both were overcome by visions of such power
They shielded their weak eyes
Against the burning dream.

They saw beyond their sight the dark frontier,
Of a cosmos, cold and comatose.
A storm of brilliant comets
Flew on wings of fire.
Earthmaker shouted to shy galaxies,
"Be born and shatter night!"

In fiery happenstance
Were born a thousand suns,
And their light fell, light-years away
Upon a solitary Troubadour walking starward
Toward waiting Terra.
The planet trembled the very instant
That the Singer's feet left atmosphere
And fell upon the desert floor.

Regis and Regina reached out to Him as He
        passed by,
Walking toward those gates
Sealed shut by rusting years.

The Singer saw a serpent rising in His path
And placed His foot upon its ugly head
Till all the writhing stopped,
And the reptile burst to flames
Beneath His feet.

Still on He walked, promethean in power,
Unto the towering gates.
He raised his hands, doubled them to fists,
And struck the ancient barriers with force.
They splintered into ruin
And fell—iron, wood and stone—in rubble.
From the long sealed-sanctuary
Eager water gushed,
As though it were alive,
Into the desert.

The vision faded.
Regina saw that it was but a dream and wept.
Regis took her in his arms
And whispered to her lost illusions,
"One day, Regina . . . . One day,
This dream is but His truth
Come early unto us
From age to age
The hope shall live until He comes."

In dimensions His two children
Would never understand,
The Father Spirit drew the blue, green planet
To His bosom and shouted to the stars,
"One day, beloved world, one day!"

A REQUIEM FOR LOVE

is a poetic narrative in the tradition of John Milton's "Paradise Lost" and J.R.R. Tolkien's Lord of the Rings Trilogy. It is the first book in Calvin Miller's new "Symphony" trilogy and will be followed by *A Symphony in Sand* and *An Overture of Light*.

Calvin Miller is a graduate of Oklahoma Baptist University and holds the Doctor of Ministries degree from Midwestern Baptist Seminary. He is senior pastor of Westside Church in Omaha, Nebraska.

Art direction, jacket design and illustration are by T.M. Williams, Design Director, Word Publishing. Chapter opening design and initial letters are by Dennis Hill, Designer-in-Chief, Word Publishing. Interior illustrations are by Rick Whipple.

A Requiem for Love was set in 11 point Goudy Roman by Publications Development Company of Crockett, Texas. Printing of book by Arcata Graphics/Fairfield, Fairfield, Pennsylvania. Jackets printed by Strine Printing Inc., York, Pennsylvania.

Books by Calvin Miller

Becoming: Yourself in the Making
Buckets of Nothing
The Finale
Guardians of the Singreale
A Hunger for Meaning
If This Be Love
The Legend of the Brotherstone
The Philippian Fragment
The Singer
The Song
Spirit, Word, and Story
Star Riders of Ren
The Table of Inwardness
The Taste of Joy
The Valiant Papers